About Me: Chris T. Risen

Hello and welcome! I'm Chris T. Risen, a seasoned professional with an extensive background in direct marketing, affiliate marketing, sales funnels, and leading dynamic sales teams. With years of invaluable experience under my belt, I've had the privilege of being a partner in one of the esteemed organizations recognized on the Inc 500 list of fastest-growing companies.

Professional Background

My journey in the dynamic field of marketing began over a decade ago, where my innate passion for connecting products with people found its true calling. Over the years, I have dedicated my skills and effort to marketing, where I've worked tirelessly to understand the intricacies and nuances that drive successful campaigns.

I've spearheaded marketing initiatives for eight distinctive brands, each with its unique identity, audience, and market position. This diversity in experience has not only broadened my perspective but also deepened my insights into the multifaceted world of marketing, making me adaptable and proficient in handling various marketing challenges and opportunities.

Expertise

Direct Marketing: With a robust background in direct marketing, I've developed and executed campaigns that directly engage the target audience, driving response and conversions through carefully crafted strategies and messages.

Affiliate Marketing: In the realm of affiliate marketing, I've worked on both sides of the spectrum—promoting products as an affiliate and driving sales through affiliates. This comprehensive experience has provided me with a deep understanding of the affiliate marketing landscape.

Sales Funnels: Mastering the art and science of sales funnels, I've successfully created and optimized conversion-focused funnels that not only attract but also retain customers, maximizing lifetime value and enhancing customer satisfaction.

Sales Teams: Leading high-performance sales teams has been one of my areas of expertise. By fostering a collaborative and motivated environment, I've guided teams to exceed sales targets while maintaining a focus on providing value to our clients and customers.

Inc 500 Fastest Growing Company Partnership: Being a partner in an Inc 500 recognized company has been a monumental milestone in my career. It is a testament to the collective hard work, innovation, and relentless pursuit of excellence that defines my approach to business and marketing.

My Approach

I approach marketing as a dynamic, evolving field that requires a blend of creativity, analytics, and an unerring focus on customer needs. In every campaign, strategy, or project I undertake, the customer is always at the core. By understanding their needs, preferences, and behaviors, I craft marketing strategies that resonate, engage, and convert.

Here's to successful marketing endeavors and the exciting journey that each campaign brings. Looking forward to crossing paths with like-minded professionals, collaborators, and enthusiasts in the field!

Chris T. Risen

Introduction: The Dawn Of AI In Business

In the data-driven epoch where data is invaluable, Artificial Intelligence (AI) stands as a paramount business instrument, orchestrating transformative shifts across diverse sectors. AI isn't simply a facet of technological progress; it's a vital catalyst for business innovation and efficacy.

AI's importance in the corporate world is undeniable. With its unmatched prowess in analyzing and deciphering extensive datasets, AI furnishes actionable insights that are integral for informed decision-making processes. From automating mundane tasks, crafting personalized customer engagements, to forecasting market trends, AI is an invaluable partner for firms seeking to sustain a competitive advantage in the rapidly evolving marketplace.

Furthermore, the adaptive nature of AI enables customization to meet the distinctive needs and goals of businesses, offering tailored solutions that directly tackle specific operational hurdles and opportunities. Through the adept utilization of AI, businesses not only enhance their current operations but are also strategically poised to identify and leverage emerging market opportunities.

Navigating Through the Guide

This book is crafted as your entry point to understanding and utilizing AI as a formidable business tool. Designed with precision, it aims to navigate you through the quintessential aspects of AI, ranging from its foundational principles to its pragmatic applications in the business sphere. Here's a concise overview of the sections contained in this guide:

Understanding the Basics of AI: Acquaint yourself with fundamental AI concepts and varieties, providing a solid foundation for confidently traversing the AI terrain.

Identifying Business Needs for AI: Discern the potential segments within your business that stand to gain significantly from AI incorporation. Master the art of conducting an accurate needs assessment to identify areas where AI can be most valuable.

Choosing the Right AI Technology: Explore the plethora of AI technologies at your disposal, grasp their respective functionalities and applications, and learn the ropes of selecting the one that resonates with your business requirements.

Implementing AI Successfully in Your Business: Gain valuable insights and strategies for a smooth AI integration process. This section will walk you through planning, risk mitigation, and team education to guarantee a triumphant AI roll-out.

Training and Maintaining AI Systems: Appreciate the importance of educating and sustaining your AI systems to ensure durability, efficiency, and compliance with ethical standards during their operation.

Measuring AI Impact and Performance: Understand the methodology for evaluating the success and influence of AI in your business through Key Performance Indicators (KPIs) and assorted performance analysis mechanisms.

Exploring Future AI Trends for Business: Stay abreast of the curve by immersing yourself in emerging AI trends and innovations, and arm yourself with knowledge on how to future-proof your enterprise in the dynamic field of AI.

Each section of this book arms you with the essential knowledge and insights needed to seamlessly incorporate AI into your business strategy, thereby unlocking unprecedented levels of efficiency, innovation, and success. Embark on this informative odyssey through the domain of AI and unearth the boundless potential it offers your business. Happy reading!

Introduction To AI

Definition

Artificial Intelligence (AI) refers to the simulation of human intelligence in machines. These machines are designed to think and act like humans by performing tasks such as learning, reasoning, problem-solving, perception, and linguistic understanding. In essence, AI is a multidisciplinary branch of science that strives to create machines capable of smart behavior.

History & Evolution

The concept of artificial beings with intelligence dates back to ancient civilizations, depicted in myths and stories of robots and automatons. However, the formal founding of AI as a scientific domain was in the mid-20th century.

Alan Turing's 1950 paper, "Computing Machinery and Intelligence," posed the question, "Can machines think?" This spurred the foundational debate of AI's potential. The first AI conference, Dartmouth Workshop in 1956, marked the birth of AI as an independent field. Over the decades, AI saw periods of optimism, funding boosts (known as the AI 'summers') and periods of disappointment and reduced funding (AI 'winters').

Recent advancements, driven by increases in computational power and data availability, have thrust AI to the forefront of technology, making what once was science fiction, a tangible reality.

Types Of AI

Narrow AI

Also known as Weak AI, Narrow AI is designed and trained for a specific task. Virtual personal assistants, such as Apple's Siri or Amazon's Alexa, are examples. They operate under a predefined set or rules and don't possess consciousness or emotions.

General AI

General AI, or Strong AI, would have all the cognitive abilities of a human being. This means it could independently perform any intellectual task that a human can. It's a more complex form of AI and remains largely theoretical, with no existing systems showcasing true General AI capabilities yet.

Superintelligent AI

A step beyond General AI, Superintelligent AI denotes a system that surpasses human intelligence across all fields, from creative endeavors to scientific reasoning. It's a topic of intense debate and speculation, as the arrival of such an AI could lead to unprecedented changes, with potential benefits and risks for humanity.

Common AI Technologies

Machine Learning

Machine Learning (ML) is a subset of AI where machines learn from data. Instead of being explicitly programmed to perform a task, they use algorithms and statistical models to identify patterns and make decisions. Common applications include recommendation systems, like those used by Netflix or Amazon.

Deep Learning

Deep Learning, a subset of ML, utilizes neural networks with many layers (hence "deep") to analyze various factors of data. It's behind many advanced AI functions, such as image and speech recognition.

NLP, Robotics, and Computer Vision

- Natural Language Processing (NLP): Allows machines to understand and respond to human language. It's the technology behind chatbots and translation services.
- Robotics: Deals with the design and creation of robots —machines that can move and react to sensory stimuli. From manufacturing robots to advanced prosthetics, the applications are vast.
- Computer Vision: Empowers machines to interpret and decide based on visual data (images, videos). Facial recognition systems and self-driving cars leverage computer vision.

Each of these technologies offers a pathway to harness the capabilities of AI, molding our modern world in myriad ways, both seen and unseen.

AI In Business Applications

Operations

AI significantly optimizes business operations, introducing efficiency and accuracy. Through predictive maintenance, AI analyzes equipment performance data to forecast potential malfunctions, reducing downtime. It also improves supply chain and inventory management by predicting demands and optimizing delivery routes.

Marketing

In marketing, AI provides invaluable customer insights, enabling personalized content delivery and engagement strategies. It automates digital marketing campaigns, implements chatbots for 24/7 customer interaction, and utilizes data analytics to identify market trends and customer behavior, making marketing efforts more effective and targeted.

Customer Service

AI enhances customer service by employing virtual assistants and chatbots, handling routine queries without human intervention. It offers personalized customer interactions and support, analyzing previous customer interactions to provide quick and efficient service, thus improving customer satisfaction and retention.

Needs Assessment: Identifying Business Areas for AI

Before implementing AI, it's crucial to identify the areas within your business that will benefit most from AI technologies.

Evaluate your business processes, pinpoint inefficiencies, and consider where automation, data analysis, or customer engagement can be enhanced with AI.

Conducting a Needs Assessment

1. **Define Objectives:** Clearly outline what you aim to achieve with AI, setting measurable goals.
2. **Analyze Processes**: Examine current business processes and identify areas where AI can offer improvements.
3. **Budget Consideration**: Understand the financial investment required and analyze the expected ROI.
4. **Skills Assessment:** Evaluate whether your team has the necessary skills or if there's a need for training or new hires.
5. **Technology Compatibility:** Ensure your existing technology infrastructure can support the AI tools you plan to implement.

Case Studies

Success Stories of AI in Business

1. **Amazon**: Amazon uses AI for product recommendations, fraud detection, and Alexa, their virtual assistant. AI analyses customer preferences, buying patterns, and searches, providing personalized recommendations, enhancing the user experience and boosting sales.
2. **Netflix**: Utilizing AI, Netflix analyses viewer preferences and watching habits. This data drives their content recommendations, and it's also employed in making decisions about which original content to produce, helping in maintaining a compelling content library that retains subscribers.
3. **American Express**: The financial services giant employs AI to analyze transactions, providing insights into customer spending habits and enabling effective fraud detection and prevention. This not only safeguards customers' assets but also offers personalized products and services.

Each case demonstrates AI's potential when correctly aligned with business needs, providing insights, improving efficiency, and ultimately contributing to significant business growth and customer satisfaction. These success stories offer valuable lessons and inspiration for any business considering AI adoption.

AI Solutions Overview

Cloud-Based AI

Cloud-based AI services provide accessibility to AI technology without the need for substantial hardware investments, making it an ideal option for small to medium enterprises (SMEs). Here are its key features:

- **Scalability:** Easily scales resources up or down based on demand, providing flexibility.
- **Cost-Effective:** Pay-as-you-use model ensures you only pay for the resources you consume.
- **Ease of Access**: Access AI resources from anywhere with an internet connection.
- **Maintenance:** The service provider manages system updates and maintenance.

On-Premise AI

On-premise AI involves housing the AI infrastructure within the physical premises of the company. This solution is often selected for its:

- **Data Security:** Enhanced control over data security and compliance.
- **Customization:** Greater freedom to customize the AI system to specific business needs.
- **Latency:** Reduced latency as data doesn't need to travel over the internet.

Choosing between cloud-based and on-premise solutions depends on your business's specific needs, including budget constraints, data security requirements, and desired level of control over the infrastructure.

Vendor Selection

Criteria for Selection

- **Experience & Expertise:** Assess the vendor's track record and proficiency in delivering AI solutions.
- **Technology Stack:** Ensure the vendor's technology aligns with your business requirements.
- **Support & Maintenance:** Consider the level of customer support and maintenance services offered.
- **Cost Structure:** Understand the pricing model and any additional costs that may arise.

Top AI Vendors Overview

- **IBM Watson:** Known for its robust AI and machine learning tools, suitable for various industries.
- **Amazon AWS:** Offers a broad set of AI services, including machine learning, chatbots, and forecasting.
- **Microsoft Azure AI:** Provides a suite of AI solutions that integrate with various Microsoft products.
- **Google Cloud AI:** Delivers AI and machine learning solutions with the backing of Google's powerful infrastructure.

Select a vendor that aligns with your business goals, operational requirements, and budget constraints.

Cost Analysis

Budgeting for AI Implementation

AI implementation involves several cost factors that businesses need to consider:

- **Software Costs:** Expenses associated with procuring the AI software or platform.
- **Hardware Expenses:** If opting for on-premise solutions, consider the cost of servers, storage, and other necessary hardware.
- **Development Costs:** Expenses incurred during the development and customization of the AI system.
- **Training & Support Costs:** Investment in training personnel to use the AI system and ongoing support costs.
  - **Maintenance & Upgrade Costs:** Budget for periodic system maintenance and future upgrades to keep the AI system running optimally.

It's essential to conduct a thorough cost analysis to prepare a realistic budget for AI implementation. Consider the total cost of ownership (TCO) and the expected return on investment (ROI) to make informed financial decisions regarding AI adoption.

Implementation Planning

Developing an AI Plan

Before delving into AI integration, a comprehensive plan must be laid out:

- **Objective Setting**: Clearly outline the goals you intend to achieve through AI.
- **Timeline Creation:** Develop a realistic timeline for implementation, including milestones and key performance indicators (KPIs).
- **Data Preparation**: Organize and clean your data. Quality data is crucial for effective AI operations.

Assigning Roles and Responsibilities

Ensure there's a dedicated team in place to oversee the AI implementation:

- **Project Manager:** Responsible for the overall implementation, ensuring it stays on schedule and within budget.
- **Data Scientist:** Works on data modeling and algorithm development.
- **Data Engineer:** Focuses on the practical application of data collection and data flows.
- **AI Ethics Officer:** Ensures the ethical considerations surrounding AI are addressed and maintained.

Risk Management

Identifying Risks

- **Data Privacy Risks:** With AI often requiring large datasets, there's a risk of data breaches or misuse.
- **Bias and Fairness Risks:** AI systems might inadvertently learn and replicate societal biases present in the training data.
- **Technology Risks:** These include system downtimes, bugs, and other technical issues.

Mitigation Strategies

- **Data Privacy Measures:** Implement robust data protection protocols.
- **Bias Audits:** Regularly audit your AI systems for bias and fairness.
- **Redundancy Plans:** Have backup systems and protocols in place for technical failures.

Team Training

AI Training Programs

Training is fundamental for your team to work effectively with the new AI tools:

- **In-House Training Programs:** Develop training modules that are specifically designed for your AI applications.
- **External Certification Courses:** Enroll your team in certification courses offered by reputable institutions or platforms.

Resources for Ongoing Learning

- **Online Platforms:** Websites and platforms offer courses on AI and machine learning, keeping your team updated with the latest skills and knowledge.
- **AI Conferences and Workshops:** These events provide insights into the latest trends and best practices in AI.
- **Community Forums and Groups:** Engage with AI communities where professionals and experts discuss and share valuable information and insights.

Investing in ongoing education ensures that your team remains proficient and updated on the latest AI technologies and practices, enabling your business to continuously benefit from AI effectively and ethically.

AI System Training

Data Collection

For AI, data is the fuel that drives performance. To initiate any AI project, amassing the right data is essential:

- **Sources of Data:** Determine where the data will be sourced. This could be from user interactions, IoT devices, third-party sources, etc.
- **Quality over Quantity**: Prioritize high-quality data over sheer volume. Consistency, relevancy, and accuracy are crucial.

Data Labeling and Preparation

After data collection, it's essential to prepare it for the training phase:

- **Data Labeling:** For supervised learning, data needs to be labeled. This might involve tagging images, categorizing content, or marking data points.
- **Data Cleaning:** Ensure the data is free from errors, duplicates, or inconsistencies that might distort AI training.
- **Data Splitting:** Reserve a portion of the data (often 20-30%) for testing and validation, ensuring that the model's learning is accurate and generalizable.

AI System Maintenance

Regular Updates

AI is not a set-it-and-forget-it tool. To stay effective, it requires frequent updates:

- **Re-training:** As new data becomes available, models might need to be re-trained to maintain or improve accuracy.
- **Algorithm Upgrades:** Stay abreast of advancements in AI and consider updating the underlying algorithms if more efficient options become available.

Troubleshooting Common Issues

- **Overfitting:** When the AI performs exceptionally well on training data but poorly on new, unseen data. Solutions include collecting more data or simplifying the model.
- **Bias:** If the AI system is producing biased outputs, it may need recalibration and a more diverse dataset.
- **Performance Issues:** Regularly monitor system performance. Any anomalies or slowdowns should be addressed promptly to ensure smooth operations.

AI Ethics And Compliance

Ensuring Ethical AI Use

With AI having the potential to impact lives, ethical considerations are paramount:

- **Transparency:** Understand and be able to explain how the AI system makes decisions.
- **Bias Prevention:** Actively work towards recognizing and eliminating biases in AI systems.
- **Respect for Privacy:** Ensure AI respects user privacy, especially when dealing with personal data.

Legal Compliance

The legal landscape around AI is rapidly evolving:

- **Data Protection Laws**: Comply with data protection regulations like GDPR or CCPA, which have implications for AI systems that handle personal data.
- **Industry-Specific Regulations:** Industries like healthcare or finance may have specific regulations concerning AI.
- **Intellectual Property**: Understand IP rights related to AI technologies and data sources.

Incorporating ethics and compliance from the start not only minimizes risks but also fosters trust among stakeholders and end-users.

Key Performance Indicators (KPI's)

Selecting and Tracking KPIs

To gauge the impact and effectiveness of AI within your business, selecting the right KPIs is vital:

- **Alignment with Business Goals:** KPIs should reflect your broader business objectives. If the goal is customer satisfaction, track metrics like response time or issue resolution rate.
- **Specificity:** Opt for clear, unambiguous KPIs. Instead of tracking "improved operations," monitor "reduced production time" or "increase in units produced per hour."
- **Measurability:** Ensure that whatever KPIs are selected can be accurately measured using available tools or data sources.
- **Regular Review:** Periodically revisit your KPIs to ensure they remain relevant as business needs and AI capabilities evolve.

Performance Analysis

Tools for AI Performance Analysis

These tools provide insights into how well the AI system is performing:

- **Data Visualization Tools:** Platforms like Tableau or PowerBI help visualize data, making it easier to identify trends, outliers, or areas of concern.
- **Custom Dashboards:** Many AI platforms come with customizable dashboards that display real-time metrics and KPIs.
- **Model Evaluation Platforms:** Tools such as TensorFlow or Scikit-learn offer built-in functionalities for model evaluation, helping assess the accuracy and efficacy of AI models.
- **A/B Testing Tools:** Compare the performance of different AI models or approaches by running them concurrently in a controlled environment.

Roi Of Ai

Calculating AI Investment Returns

Understanding the ROI of AI implementation provides a clear picture of its financial impact:

- **Direct Financial Gains:** Calculate the direct revenue or savings generated through AI, whether through increased sales, reduced operational costs, or other tangible financial benefits.
- **Indirect Benefits**: These might include enhanced customer satisfaction, brand reputation, or employee productivity, which can lead to long-term financial gains.
- **Total Cost:** Account for all expenses related to AI, including software costs, hardware investments, training, maintenance, and any associated overheads.
- **ROI Formula:**

$$ROI = \left(\frac{\text{Net Profit from AI}}{\text{Total Cost of AI Implementation}} \right) \times 100$$

Monitor ROI over time to understand the long-term value and impact of your AI investments, adjusting strategies as needed for optimal financial returns.

AI Innovations

Emerging Technologies in AI

The realm of AI is fast-evolving, with new technologies pushing the boundaries of what's possible:

- **Quantum Computing:** The union of quantum mechanics and computing promises to boost AI capabilities exponentially. Quantum algorithms can process vast amounts of data and complex computations much faster than traditional digital methods.
- **Neurosymbolic AI:** A blend of symbolic AI and neural networks, it's believed to bridge the gap between human-like understanding and machine learning, enabling machines to reason more like humans.
- **Federated Learning:** This approach allows machines to learn from data stored on multiple devices, enhancing data privacy. It's particularly beneficial in scenarios like healthcare, where data privacy is paramount.
- **Generative Adversarial Networks (GANs):** These are designed for unsupervised machine learning, where one network generates data and another evaluates it. It's finding applications in image creation, style transfers, and more.

Ethical AI

Importance of Ethical Considerations

As AI's role in society grows, so does the urgency of ethical considerations:

- **Bias & Fairness:** AI systems are only as unbiased as the data they're trained on. Ensuring fairness requires conscious efforts to remove biases from training data and algorithms.
- **Transparency & Explainability:** As decisions made by AI have far-reaching implications, it's crucial for AI systems to operate transparently and provide explanations for their decisions.
- **Accountability:** Establishing clear lines of accountability ensures that when AI systems err, there's a system in place to address issues and prevent future occurrences.
- **Privacy & Data Rights:** With AI often relying on large datasets, ensuring the privacy of individuals and respecting data rights becomes paramount.

Future-Proofing Your Business

Staying Ahead in AI Developments

As AI continues its forward march, businesses must be prepared:

- **Continuous Learning:** Encourage a culture of continuous learning. As AI evolves, so should the knowledge and understanding of your team.

- **Collaborate with AI Communities:** Engage with AI researchers, developers, and enthusiasts. Partnerships with academic institutions or AI startups can offer fresh perspectives and insights.
- **Invest in R&D:** Allocate resources for AI research and development. Experimenting with new AI technologies can yield innovative solutions and offer competitive advantages.
- **Stay Updated with Regulations:** As governments and international bodies formulate new regulations surrounding AI, ensure that your business remains compliant to avoid potential legal pitfalls.

Staying proactive, rather than reactive, will position your business to harness the full potential of AI, both now and in the unforeseeable future.

Resources

Further Reading and Learning Resources

To deepen your understanding of AI, consider the following authoritative texts and resources:

- **"Artificial Intelligence: Structures and Strategies for Complex Problem Solving" by George F. Luger:** An excellent resource for grasping the foundational principles of AI.
- **"Artificial Intelligence: A Guide to Intelligent Systems" by Michael Negnevitsky:** Offers clear explanations of AI technologies and their applications.
- **"AI Superpowers: China, Silicon Valley, and the New World Order" by Kai-Fu Lee:** Provides insights into the global AI landscape.
- **"Machine Learning Yearning" by Andrew Ng:** A crucial guide for those involved in the technical development of machine learning systems.

Online Courses and Certifications on AI

- **Coursera:** Offers courses and certifications from top universities and companies.
- **Udacity:** Provides nanodegree programs in AI and machine learning.
- **edX:** Hosts AI courses from universities like Harvard, MIT, and more.
- **LinkedIn Learning:** Offers a variety of courses to improve your AI and machine learning skills.

These platforms offer extensive learning materials and certifications that can augment your knowledge and expertise in